CW01306641

Contended Being

CONTENDED BEING

Rachel Downing

authorHOUSE®

AuthorHouse™ UK
1663 Liberty Drive
Bloomington, IN 47403 USA
www.authorhouse.co.uk
Phone: UK TFN: 0800 0148641 (Toll Free inside the UK)
UK Local: (02) 0369 56322 (+44 20 3695
6322 from outside the UK)

Copyright © 2024 Rachel Downing. All rights reserved.

No part of this book may be reproduced, stored in a retrieval system, or transmitted by any means without the written permission of the author.

Published by AuthorHouse 06/03/2024

ISBN: 979-8-8230-8663-9 (sc)
ISBN: 979-8-8230-8664-6 (e)

Library of Congress Control Number: 2024905209

CIP catalogue record for this book is available from the British Library.

Print information available on the last page.

Getty Stock Images. Creative ID: 914381762

Any people depicted in stock imagery provided by Getty Images are models, and such images are being used for illustrative purposes only. Certain stock imagery © Getty Images.

This book is printed on acid-free paper.

Because of the dynamic nature of the Internet, any web addresses or links contained in this book may have changed since publication and may no longer be valid. The views expressed in this work are solely those of the author and do not necessarily reflect the views of the publisher, and the publisher hereby disclaims any responsibility for them.

INTRODUCTION

"eschatology"

n. the branch of theology or biblical exegesis concerned with the end of the world.

[C19: from the Greek *eskhatos* last.]

Collins English Dictionary, 1995.

"To recognise untruth as a condition of life – that certainly means resisting accustomed value feelings in a dangerous way; and a philosophy that risks this would by that token alone place itself beyond good and evil."

[Friedrich Nietzsche, Beyond Good and Evil.]

*"Indeed, when the water (of the Deluge)
overflowed the limit,
We carried you in the floating Ark."*

Quran, The Concrete Reality, 69:11.

"My child, let your tears flow for the dead."

Book of Sirach, Ecclesiasticus, 38: 16-23.

CONTENTS

Introduction vii
Prologue 19

CONFUSIONS

1. In Opposition 23
2. Now We Are Waken 24
3. Did That Not Happen 25
4. She Knew Her Own Loss 26
5. Then She Said To Herself 27

CREDENCE

6. The Gateway To Absence 31
7. I Am Falling 32
8. This Is What We Did Not Share 33
9. Without Alarm 34
10. The Morning Light Was Distant 35

THE CRY

11.	He Says Fall Away With Me	39
12.	She Also Means It Is To Know	40
13.	She Wonders Why	41
14.	They Turn Towards Her	42

MANTLE

15.	Liminal And Powerless	45
16.	Pity Or Goodness	46
17.	I Did Not Know That	47
18.	In These Moments Of Quiet	48
19.	Laud The Common Earth	49
20.	Because It Is The Sacrilege	50

LAMENT

21.	Across The World	53
22.	Anguish And Trauma	54
23.	And Shall We Take This	55
24.	You Will Survive	56
25.	Look They Led Me There	57
26.	And She Saw God Was Angry	58

BEREFT

27. Reflections	61
28. Literal And Concrete	62
29. In This Flight	63
30. Unlifted In Resilience	64
31. No Paradox	65
32. Reminded Suddenly	66

PRAGMATISM

33. She Walks	69
34. We Did Not Walk	70
35. To This Day	71
36. Presence	72
37. Loss Echoing Loss	73

Acknowledgements	77
The Author	79
Other Books by Rachel Downing	81
Editorial Review: 'The Rainstorm'	83

PROLOGUE

Contended Being is a poetic portrayal echoing loss stylised in the form of lament. The story begins in deceptive simplicity of possibility and prayer, and ends in tensions of betrayal; at once, both striking in narration and fearful in interpretation.

Rachel Downing,
Somerset, 2024.

Part I.

Confusions

1. <u>In Opposition</u>

In opposition
she did not hear and she hears
theirs the means, lifeworld transmitted
and herein the unreason, time trapped
transitional
perceptions act and actions
non-self or contended being, fallen,
and so she summoned strength
as they chose to replicate mirrors
mimetic, of normative example
of shared commonality and by example,
submission. Chance
the paradigm of the unity:
unknown, unagreed, and revised?

2. <u>Now We Are Waken</u>

Now we are waken
in minds divisible
in language of dreams,
variations and presence
of archaic thinking
speaks pictures and words;
they appeared to her without flowers
and she is puzzled, an imaginary freedom
bereft, and devastate
our loss, just not this fight;
feel an immediate anger, fear
abandoned to explain, and false sense
to the beginnings of thought
preserved in dreams, echoing
loss resonating grief
and she wishes she could return
to the simple past tense.

3. Did That Not Happen

Did that not happen.
Connections of ideas
nonstatus and deceptions,
in an instance, such loss. And they said,
let me see unforgiving.
And there they had stood
unambiguously with council in assimilation
and she was lost amidst them
in vague recognition to them
derived from effort to be fully present.
She thinks again
the human condition of experience
plausible, tangible, to be fluently true,
number or name,
and so she gathered her papers
rushing outdoors over the threshold,
gathered in thinking, awe, and anticipation,
waiting sensibly for those living spirits to
leave.

4. She Knew Her Own Loss

She knew her own loss,
they had collective self
to escape ingrained rumination,
so she follows imploding silence
along wildflower pathways
before the distant shading light canopies,
thoughts surrounded,
she worked through the lines
trailing, unfair, inconsistent, if I am safe
and if only to have meant,
matriarchal subsets.
Without requests
enactments ran through her
and if lives co-existed as one,
she who decided and trespassed,
caught consciousness
to watch them defend.
And then they reached the shore,
unblended waves of poise, and rage,
astounded.

5. Then She Said To Herself

Then she said to herself,
this is my best life and my future,
write as both subject and clause
and the spaces between words
against dissociation, be kind,
in style consciously mundane,
a better window to the world,
and the knell
not to speak,
demand avoidance,
unreality to escape participation,
and she hears only, to have life,
feelings surface and she is shocked,
let me belong, there is no equivalence.
Then how difficult is it to fail absence?

Part II.

Credence

6. <u>The Gateway To Absence</u>

The gateway to absence.
And grief
caused them to be filled with feelings,
resentment and negation.
She stood unaware and targeted.
And she also
knew a myriad of limitations
as she unclasped her hands
indecisively
to prepare the tablescape.
Still resilient.
He did not stay
to see the land was already frozen.

7. <u>I Am Falling</u>

'I am falling
I need to be carried, I am broken.'
The earth prepared necessary.
'The coffin carried
walked through the burial flight
shroud in daylight, rest in the shadows.'
Such is the encompassing sadness
and because I asked for more
help me or help them better.
'Who will be their guide
which words, which nouns in declension
and infinite deceptions?'
The decision
for your sake, reconciliation the burden
historical knowledge.
'Then how did we learn to make claim.'

8. <u>This Is What We Did Not Share</u>

This is what we did not share
and to know when to stay away
to let the boundaries to God,
this is your home, this is my home,
or take to your boundaries, leave me,
lay down your anger.
Live lament.
She heard and she wanted to scream.
As we saw a book lay on a coffin,
pages flutter,
in apparition, illusion, truth,
phenomenon,
discernment and discretion.
See now. Hear now. Know now.

9. <u>Without Alarm</u>

Without alarm
and because the superstitious
did not cost effort,
law and politic, attentive
and so long adapted to her altered state,
she thinks she sees,
she thinks she knows
and in deference, she guesses
external others
whilst only some may know natural
variations and minds selected,
subject and predicate
and none,
structural and substantive delineated.

10. <u>The Morning Light Was Distant</u>

The morning light was distant,
the evening light closer,
home again safely
and warmer beside the open fire
she finds comfort in glowing embers;
then she holds the other book
under polemic dead-letters, guided
such a decision
looking through the windows
faint grey mist seems to fill the room,
then the room slowly darkened,
before she is sleeping.

Part III.

The Cry

11. <u>He Says Fall Away With Me</u>

He says, fall away with me.
His words forge a shield.
They wanted her to sit, in belief.
When I did not want my heart to fail
in fear and sadness,
then, life less
concrete unnamed, not as aggressive
those ancestors, this close, cry earth
and they knew the slate discouraged.
'For how did we defer the reckoning?'

12. <u>She Also Means It Is To Know</u>

She also means it is to know
the dramatic power, the word humanity,
and it takes a second age for her to accept
she could be an old woman.
News set low in the background
she does not know
how to ask again, this counselling,
or how she will meet it,
her resilience waning.
Unvaried, forbidden
and she is shy of conversation
and they do not trust promise.

13. She Wonders Why

She wonders why
there is no call, waiting days
celebrate, then she would be happy,
except now days have become night
and night has become day
and still the tireless trauma
finds expression and she feels weighted
and cannot lift herself to move through
the crumbling immensity of sadness,
and she does not want another day,
this being, and all along dear kindness
danced with her maybe
before I was buried
the earth cry echoed
plainly the levels of language.

14. They Turn Towards Her

They turn towards her
as she reaches the door.
When they speak, subliminal cuts metal.
Be free from fear,
there is comfort and victory in recovery,
she thinks.
And she sees their reflections,
adults, sound in purpose and reason,
not afraid to fail.
All we have is our conscious self,
she wants to say.

Part IV.

Mantle

15. Liminal And Powerless

Liminal and powerless.
They did not want to take criticism,
allegiances, years of complicity,
not the annoyance
nor the intimidation in immediacy evoked.
Patient, objectified.
When they spoke,
how it is not to feel safe.
He said he would go.
So many journeys. Gone.
Conceit and rights.
Ritual and sacrifice.
A time to mourn.

16. Pity Or Goodness

Pity or goodness
assuming purpose enabling appeal
haunting daily living and foreboding,
as she feared her impulsivity
she mourned the waste of years and ideas,
the loss of originality
and how she had squandered
her consciousness;
and the good land saw
and nature responded in signs and symbols;
months passed in seasons of intuitive
contrasts,
the vast sky, gentle sun, gentle rain,
and those stones
not lifted to the hightide banks.
And how shall we sing in exile?
But they drew back and waited.

17. I Did Not Know That

I did not know that.
Calls ended abruptly,
mixed and demanding,
they were animated,
they were saying, validate me.
More recently, there were silences,
planned interruption,
a waiting tactic to please repeat that,
she was sorry,
as she cowered in anticipation
and because she could not cope,
take faulted endurance,
oppose the chaos,
those permissions deflecting
that are so difficult to dispel.

18. In These Moments Of Quiet

In these moments of quiet
and there are glimpses,
the kindness and connection
but the offerings are unaccepted.
A structure is built. No. Then not.
Sacrilege deconstructed,
countable nouns eradicated
and chaos over water.
And how not to see those incidents
as the common markers, of potentiality,
of one shared God and of one shared world
of future to share
or, as the deficiencies inherent in language,
and the meaning of words
and symbolism through time.

19. Laud The Common Earth

Laud the common earth.
Land, folk culture or ignorance of.
Even closeness is solitary. Cold.
And then the next day and the next
extreme, loneliness
and solitary
deprivation resounded
and impacted,
disabling her, of days, of the years.
An impersonal deity.
Assumption, myth and labels.
She is mother sister daughter friend.
Such is a war of claims, and seal.
Laud the common earth.

20. <u>Because It Is The Sacrilege</u>

Because it is the sacrilege
that has already happened,
knowledge already failed,
and because the rebounding spirits
have already caught up to each
of her people
in retaliation, without mercy
to each of us according to our age.

Part V.

Lament

21. Across The World

Across the world,
the word no is hollow.
On a new altar,
retaliation, acts, books, and conscience,
all were burnt in sacrifice.
Anger overwhelms me.
And then the zeitgeist spoke,
and said:
'So you know what it is to suffer.'

22. Anguish And Trauma

Anguish and trauma,
there is a gap in the middle of my body
encompassing
my cry and my feelings,
the cry for recognition,
and I do not want betrayal
and I am judge.
And the world looks on.

23. And Shall We Take This

And shall we take this
away from humankind
so there is only knowledge
for right and wrong
of those women
and of those men
who took away all that is mother,
of the God who left me
standing alone to suffer
without peace, in violence,
without knowing how not to hurt another?

CONTENDED BEING   Lament

24. You Will Survive

You will survive.
And if I do not care
and if there is nothing more to be done.
And if there is something more to say.
And you cannot hear me screaming.
I weep regret and sorrow
for time when life was wrong,
and I weep in plea for time
when people were only good,
and because it is my heart
that cried out for the borders.

25. Look They Led Me There

Look they led me there
and God left me there so you would know,
she said.
They took me there and gave me food.
They gave me food and I ate, she tells.
And when we are lost,
shall we show you in the wrong way
the scenes, and how we are lost, or
who will tell you
because we are in fear
and because we know you already know?
Shall I regret? You are to believe me.

26. And She Saw God Was Angry

And she saw God was angry
when she thought:
when anger at wrong consumes me,
help them, not me, Lord.
Feel now the pain, my hands
as I hold them flat to the wooden table
so that I cannot write,
so that I cannot hurt again,
tone, intonation, imitation.
Resonating grief.

Part VI.

Bereft

27. Reflections

Reflections,
she had dared to walk
through the rooms between them,
contradictions, companionship, antinomies;
the tight hold and the slight,
offer of ephemeral others
had kept her so quietly in near time,
clear apparent moments visible.
Is it not real,
their walk in rhetoric,
and the reality
impinged solid ground,
and who will convey a life in truth
in this the plurality of her sentence?
Light lines
between necessity and past sacrifice.

28. Literal And Concrete

Literal and concrete
storm rain melancholy loneliness,
her body walked away from her heart,
she made herself leave,
first in denial then in defence
and then in failure,
there was nowhere,
she was determined,
she listened so intently,
she counted many chances,
she had asked again.

29. In This Flight

In this flight,
penitence,
they could never have. Be to them, and
would one more word, one more prayer
for her calmness
over which her own constancy prevailed;
and she delays her return,
the tracks are not long enough,
she takes smaller steps,
she walks and walks over the vales
in the cold night air,
stars in blackness,
and she wishes she could stay,
feel safe for longer
then to go back to own self.
Make sense of the stories.

30. <u>Unlifted In Resilience</u>

Unlifted in resilience
she unpacks, room to room,
waves crashing the monotony of death.
She takes time to rest, found dress
to reject the voices, impersonal weakness,
existential risk,
reason enough to obscure herself mute
and how many layers of identity
and they had chattered noisily
as her own thoughts surrounded
her own pragmatic silence.

31. No Paradox

No paradox,
this is enough, she mutters.
For the ancestors.
She shivered, wrapped the woollen shawl
around her herself,
folding her arms
she walked to the windows
looking out, the summer storm
swarming clouds of greys,
deep dark blues and blackness.
And faintly, she prays.
Between me and each madness,
the life of God breathe.

32. Reminded Suddenly

Reminded suddenly
in relief for the curdled biographies
held their lives of human potential,
a reach to pathos, deaths carried back
to atoms, sparks of memories
could never exceed
neither compassion nor irritability,
a claim to an unfaulted unfaltering
narration.
At the window ledge
leaning back into the cold enclave
she sees past sheltered sand,
gathering clouds descending;
the land would contain the storm
and the vastness of the level seascape
with her in renewal.
Presence be the love of God
with me when I die.

Part VII.

Pragmatism

33. She Walks

She walks
and until through the ages of the seasons,
and she is alone
barefoot on the summer sand,
sun hat in one hand,
sandals in the other,
and she walks over the sandbanks
winding through the meadow
to the edge of the seashore,
and as always
walking through those moments
she sings freely, rhymes of the ancients
and new. Purpose and repentance.
Leave me my reading,
reason these lines leading.

34. We Did Not Walk

We did not walk
towards her alone,
said the living forces.
Render unto him…,
in syntax and linguistics,
she may have said.
Here, the betrayal at her birth.
For the imposition
and the sharing of the sacred,
the *fractalled* self,
ideas as living structures.
And too much to know?
Denotation and connotation.
Unity and separation.
Separation loss,
bound existence in communion.

35. To This Day

To this day
affected by suggestion,
around and around minds
like that day the nightmare strikes
as she remembers
once more, light and darkness,
and she knows something more,
how silent the conscious self
and she is crushed in horror;
it is impossible to bear
and the knowledge of sin
and opposing thoughts;
and it is impossible to run away.
He judged disunity.

36. <u>Presence</u>

Presence
in consciousness broken
and she knows it is a form of death,
even one part of such existence
and still, she is unaware
or unable or unwilling
because experience has taught her that;
and, this being created, and primal mind:
compromised, restrained, vital
love and loss.

37. Loss Echoing Loss

Loss echoing loss
resonating grief.
Words in existence. Nouns of sacrifice.
She looks back,
the fatal demand for mind over body
the wounding affect to her system,
temporal, and logic.
Then she waits for the pages
written in structures, eternally woven,
to flutter and settle, mottled,
floating on the still surface water
as the boat falls to the flowers.
Footsteps, on the cold saltwater sea.
Waiting.
She is silt and clay and sand and stone.

The End

ACKNOWLEDGEMENTS

Writing is creative therapy and I am happy to share. This book is to some extent in memory of my mother and my grandmother. I am grateful to my children and to AuthorHouse for their help in making this publication possible.

THE AUTHOR

I am a woman of mixed religious and cultural heritages.

I have a BA in Modern European History from the University of East Anglia, Norfolk; and I live in Somerset, UK.

Other Books by Rachel Downing

The Rainstorm

(AuthorHouse Bookstore & Amazon)

RACHEL DOWNING
THE RAINSTORM

'The mysterious free verses collected in *The Rainstorm* explore the power of language and the paradoxes of the self.'

'Throughout, *The Rainstorm* explores the often conflicting aspects of a single consciousness using enigmatic images. Some may experience the poems' abstractions as invitations to multiple readings, used to construct a logical, spiritual, or emotional sensibility; often, though, the book seems to be a private communication with one's self.'

Forward & Clarion Editorial Review, Michele Sharpe.

****
~~~~~~~~~~~~~~~~~~~~~~~~~~~~~~~~~~~~

****
~~~~~~~~~~~~~~~~~~~~~~~~~~~~~~~~~~~~

****
~~~~~~~~~~~~~~~~~~~~~~~~~~~~~~~~~~~~